T0011172

TWO TRUTHS AND A MYTH

King Tut's TOMB

SPOT THE MYTHS

by Carol Kim

Published by Capstone Press, an imprint of Capstone
1710 Roe Crest Drive, North Mankato, Minnesota 56003
capstonepub.com

Copyright © 2024 by Capstone. All rights reserved. No part of this
publication may be reproduced in whole or in part, or stored in a
retrieval system, or transmitted in any form or by any means, electronic,
mechanical, photocopying, recording, or otherwise, without written
permission of the publisher.

Library of Congress Cataloging-in-Publication Data is available
on the Library of Congress website.
ISBN: 9781669062547 (hardcover)
ISBN: 9781669062622 (paperback)
ISBN: 9781669062615 (ebook PDF)

Summary: The 1922 discovery of King Tut's tomb is one of the most
important ancient Egyptian finds in history. People have told stories
about it ever since. Read some of the stories. Then see if you can separate
the myths from the truths.

Editorial Credits
Editor: Carrie Sheely; Designer: Bobbie Nuytten; Media Researcher:
Rebekah Hubstenberger; Production Specialist: Whitney Schaefer

Image Credits
Alamy: Barry Iverson, 18, Danita Delimont, 25, North Wind Picture
Archives, 9, The Print Collector, 7; Associated Press: Amr Nabil, 13;
Getty Images: Brandon Rosenblum, 23, Culture Club, 4, Grafissimo, 8,
Historica Graphica Collection/Heritage Images, 21 (top), Hulton Archive,
Cover, 14, 28, Khaled DESOUKI/AFP, 26, Scott Olson, 29, Universal
History Archive/Universal Images Group, 17; Newscom: imageBROKER/
Raimund Franken, 13; Shutterstock: Apostrophe, design element
(texture), Everett Collection, 11, Jaroslav Moravcik, 21 (bottom right),
Tasha Romart, design element (icons); The Metropolitan Museum of Art:
Purchase, Edward S. Harkness Gift, 1926, 22

All internet sites appearing in back matter were available and accurate
when this book was sent to press.

Printed and bound in the USA. PO 5626

TABLE OF CONTENTS

A Tomb of Treasures 4

The Boy King 6

The Tomb 10

The Discovery 14

The Mummy 18

Death of the King 22

The Artifacts 26

Glossary 30
Read More 31
Internet Sites 31
Index 32
About the Author 32

Words in **bold** are in the glossary.

Treasures

Tutankhamun was an ancient Egyptian king, or pharaoh. For more than 3,000 years, his tomb lay undisturbed deep underground. That changed when English **archaeologist** Howard Carter uncovered the tomb in Egypt's Valley of the Kings in 1922.

King Tutankhamun is also known as King Tut. He was not well known before his tomb was discovered. The remarkable treasures found inside his tomb made King Tut a famous pharaoh.

A sculpture of King Tut's head was found in the entrance to the pharaoh's tomb.

Scientists have closely studied King Tut and his tomb for more than 100 years. But people continue to believe many myths about them. Follow along to explore the facts and myths. Three statements will be presented together. One is a myth or **misconception**. Can you separate the myth from the facts?

HOW CAN I TELL WHAT'S TRUTH AND WHAT'S A MYTH?

START HERE. ⇨ Does the statement include words like "all" or "none"?

YES ⇨ It might be a myth. Words such as "all" or "none" often simplify complicated topics. These statements might not be true.

NO ⇨ Does the statement include specific information, such as names or dates?

YES ⇨ It might be true. Details are important when dealing with facts. The more details a statement provides, the more likely it is to be true.

NO ⇨ It might be a myth. Vague facts without detail might be made up. It's good to question statements that don't include specific details.

The Boy King

TRUTH OR MYTH?

1. KING TUT DID LITTLE DURING HIS REIGN THAT HAD ANY LONG-TERM EFFECTS ON EGYPTIAN LIFE.

King Tut was Egypt's ruler for a relatively short amount of time, about 10 years. His father, Akhenaten, was pharaoh for 17 years. Some pharaohs ruled for much longer. King Tut's short reign affected how much he was able to accomplish. It didn't have lasting effects.

2. KING TUT WAS ONLY 9 YEARS OLD WHEN HE ASCENDED TO THE THRONE.

King Tut was born around 1341 BCE. Akhenaten died in 1336 BCE. Tutankhamun was young. At the time, his name was Tutankhaten. He took over as king when he was 9.

3. LEADERS WHO CAME AFTER KING TUT REMOVED HIS NAME FROM MANY OFFICIAL RECORDS. HE WAS ALMOST COMPLETELY FORGOTTEN UNTIL THE DISCOVERY OF HIS TOMB.

Before the reign of Akhenaten, Egypt had been a very rich and powerful country. But while Akhenaten was king, it began to show signs of decline.

Akhenaten

For hundreds of years, Egyptians worshipped many gods. When he became king, Akhenaten allowed people to worship only the sun god Aten. He also moved the capital from Thebes to Amarna.

Rulers who came after King Tut believed Akhenaten's changes hurt Egypt. They tried to erase Akhenaten from history as well as King Tut. Their names were removed from official lists of kings. Tut's name was even chiseled off all his statues.

THE MYTH

KING TUT DID LITTLE DURING HIS REIGN THAT HAD ANY LONG-TERM EFFECTS ON EGYPTIAN LIFE.

After the death of his father, King Tut was aware of how unpopular some of his father's actions were. He reversed many of his father's changes. He allowed people to worship many gods again. He moved the capital back to Thebes. Temples and palaces were rebuilt. His decisions helped rebuild Egypt's **economy**.

A pharaoh and other ancient Egyptians worship the god Sobek.

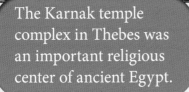

The Karnak temple complex in Thebes was an important religious center of ancient Egypt.

9

TRUTH OR MYTH?

1. KING TUT'S TOMB IS SMALLER THAN THOSE OF OTHER PHARAOHS.

The thousands of items in King Tut's tomb included clothes, jewelry, large furniture pieces, and six **chariots**. But the tomb is small for a pharaoh. King Tut may have died unexpectedly. It is possible there wasn't time to prepare a larger tomb.

2. THERE ARE SECRET ROOMS IN KING TUT'S TOMB THAT HAVE NOT YET BEEN UNCOVERED.

In 2014, the wall surfaces inside King Tut's tomb were scanned. Egyptologist Dr. Nicholas Reeves studied the images. He suggested the images showed outlines of sealed doorways that led to hidden rooms. He also said Egyptian queen Nefertiti could be buried in one of the hidden rooms.

3. KING TUT'S TOMB IS MADE UP OF FOUR ROOMS AND A CORRIDOR. THE ROOMS ARE AN ANNEX, ANTECHAMBER, TREASURY, AND BURIAL CHAMBER.

After going down the steps to the first door, there is a corridor that leads to a second door. It opens to the antechamber. It is the first room filled with treasures. The next room is the annex. The burial chamber is where the remains of King Tut were found. The treasury was filled with many items, including the **embalmed** organs of King Tut.

Artifacts from King Tut's tomb

FACT

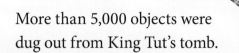

More than 5,000 objects were dug out from King Tut's tomb.

THE MYTH

THERE ARE SECRET ROOMS IN KING TUT'S TOMB THAT HAVE NOT YET BEEN UNCOVERED.

Between 2015 and 2018, people did three more scans of the tomb walls. In 2018, 40 scans were taken. For the most part, experts decided the scans did not show any **evidence** of hidden rooms. Dr. Reeves later said he may still be correct. But most experts do not agree.

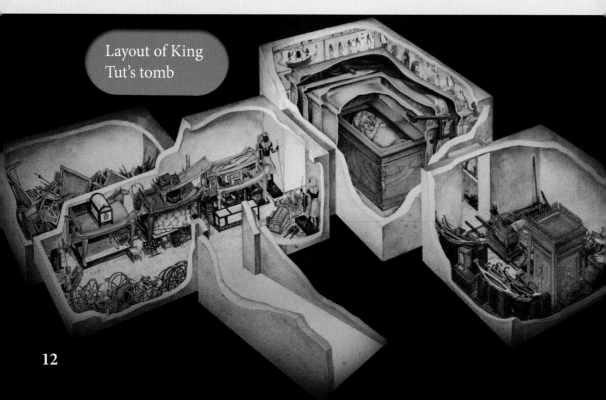

Layout of King Tut's tomb

An expert scans a wall in the tomb's burial chamber in 2016.

The Discovery

1. HOWARD CARTER WAS THE ONE TO DISCOVER THE STEPS THAT LED TO THE TOMB.

Howard Carter had a team of local Egyptian workers helping him search for King Tut's tomb. They had to clear tons of rock and debris.

Lord Carnarvon was Carter's sponsor. He provided the money for the search. In October 1922, Carnarvon was ready to give up the search. But Carter convinced him to keep going.

Carter and his team worked even harder. In November, Carter discovered the tomb steps by chance.

Howard Carter (right) walks alongside Lord Carnarvon in the Valley of the Kings in 1922.

2. AFTER UNCOVERING THE STEPS TO THE TOMB, CARTER HAD TO COVER THEM UP AND WAIT FOR LORD CARNARVON TO ARRIVE.

Carter and his team dug until they uncovered 16 steps and reached the top part of a door.

At that point, Carter reburied the door and steps. He sent a message to Carnarvon, telling him of the discovery. Then he had to wait. It took more than two weeks for Carnarvon to travel to Egypt. After he arrived, Carter was able to start digging again.

3. HOWARD CARTER WAS NOT THE FIRST TO ENTER KING TUT'S TOMB SINCE HIS BURIAL.

Howard Carter was the first person to uncover King Tut's tomb in modern times. As he dug, he saw signs that robbers had entered the tomb earlier. The signs suggested that robbers had broken in not long after King Tut's burial.

Carter discovered that the upper left corner of the door to the tomb had been opened and resealed at least twice. Fortunately, the robbers had not gone farther than the antechamber.

15

THE MYTH

HOWARD CARTER WAS THE ONE TO DISCOVER THE STEPS THAT LED TO THE TOMB.

Howard Carter had a team of workers helping him search for King Tut's tomb. Some historians believe it was the team's water boy, Hussein Abd el-Rassul, who discovered the staircase. Carter was not even at the dig site at the time.

Some stories say that on the morning of November 4, 1922, Hussein brought jars of water for the workers. While placing the jars in the sand, his hand brushed against some stone. Looking closer, he found the top of a step cut into the ground. When Carter arrived later, the workers were waiting to show him what Hussein had found.

Hussein Abd el-Rassul wears a necklace from the tomb.

The Mummy

1. HOWARD CARTER HAD TO REMOVE KING TUT'S BODY FROM THE COFFIN IN PIECES, INCLUDING CUTTING THE HEAD OFF AT THE NECK.

As part of the burial process, oils had been poured all over King Tut's body. The oils had hardened. They kept King Tut's body firmly glued inside. Howard Carter tried to soften the sticky layer, but nothing worked.

He had no choice but to remove the mummy from the coffin in pieces. His team had to cut the head off at the neck. They also separated the pelvis from the trunk and detached the arms and legs.

King Tut's mummy

2. KING TUT'S MUMMY CAUGHT FIRE AFTER HIS BURIAL.

Egyptologist Chris Naunton studied some remains of King Tut under a powerful microscope. There were signs the remains had been burned. He believed the embalming oils used had a chemical reaction. This caused the mummy to start on fire.

3. A "MUMMY'S CURSE" WAS BEHIND THE DEATHS OF SEVERAL PEOPLE INVOLVED IN OPENING KING TUT'S TOMB.

Lord Carnarvon died less than five months after opening King Tut's tomb. Soon, people began saying his death was caused by a "mummy's **curse**."

Some newspapers reported a curse was found written on a clay tablet just outside King Tut's tomb. Other reports said more than 12 mysterious deaths could be linked to the curse. They included Lord Carnarvon's half-brother Aubrey Herbert and a wealthy railroad executive named George Jay Gould. Both deaths took place within a year after the tomb's discovery.

THE MYTH

A "MUMMY'S CURSE" WAS BEHIND THE DEATHS OF SEVERAL PEOPLE INVOLVED IN OPENING KING TUT'S TOMB.

Stories of a written curse turned out to be untrue. Reporters had spread rumors of a supposed curse to stir up the interest of readers.

The deaths said to be linked to the mummy's curse were not from mysterious causes. Lord Carnarvon cut a mosquito bite on his face with a razor. The cut developed into a blood infection, which led to his death. Carnarvon had also been in poor health for years.

Only six of the 26 people who were at the tomb's opening had died within 10 years. Howard Carter lived for another 17 years.

Lord Carnarvon leads a group of people invited to the unofficial opening of King Tut's tomb.

FACT

A guard watching over King Tut's funerary mask on display in San Francisco claimed a mild stroke was caused by the "mummy's curse." He tried to get payment for his health issue. But a judge threw out the claim.

Death of the King

1. KING TUT WAS MURDERED BY A BLOW TO THE HEAD.

In 1968, researchers took an X-ray of King Tut's mummy. They found some small bone fragments inside King Tut's skull. It showed that King Tut had been killed by a blow to the back of his head.

2. KING TUT WAS BURIED WITH SMALL FIGURINES MEANT TO ACT AS SERVANTS IN THE AFTERLIFE.

Ancient Egyptians believed in an afterlife. King Tut's tomb included hundreds of small figurines called shabtis. Carved into some of the figures was a magical spell. It told a shabti to work for the king in the afterlife.

Shabti

3. THE TOMB WAS PREPARED IN A HURRY AND SEALED BEFORE THE PAINT WAS DRY ON THE WALLS.

King Tut's death may have taken everyone by surprise. Usually the tombs of pharaohs took many years to prepare. But for King Tut, many items had not been crafted yet.

There are spots of mold on the painted walls inside the tomb. The mold formed because the paint was not yet dry when the tomb was sealed. This helps prove the burial was rushed.

The painted walls of King Tut's burial chamber show his journey into the afterlife.

THE MYTH

KING TUT WAS MURDERED BY A BLOW TO THE HEAD.

In 2005, experts performed a CT scan of King Tut's mummy. These scans produce more detailed images than X-rays. The scan proved that the skull damage happened after King Tut's death. It was either caused during the mummification process or when Howard Carter removed King Tut from his coffin.

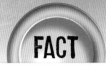

FACT

Experts believe the most likely cause of King Tut's death was either from an infection from a broken leg or malaria. Malaria is a disease that mosquitoes can carry and give to people.

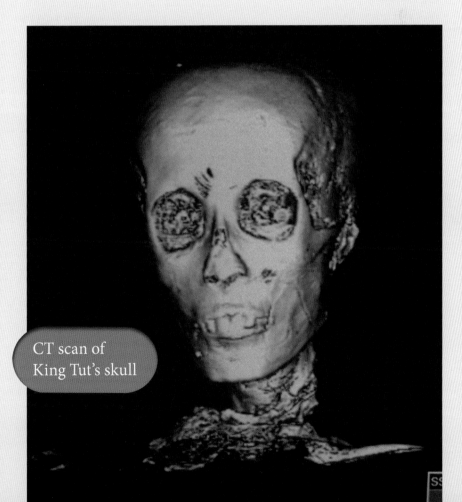

CT scan of King Tut's skull

The Artifacts

1. IMAGES OF KING TUT'S ENEMIES WERE ON THE SOLES OF HIS SANDALS. ANCIENT EGYPTIANS THOUGHT THIS WOULD ALLOW KING TUT TO STEP ON THE FACES OF HIS ENEMIES WHENEVER HE WALKED IN THE AFTERLIFE.

The **artifacts** in the tomb included at least 80 pairs of footwear. The soles of some sandals had images of King Tut's enemies.

Copies of sandals found in King Tut's tomb

2. ROBBERS WERE THE ONLY ONES TO TAKE ITEMS FROM KING TUT'S TOMB AFTER HIS BURIAL.

Items were almost certainly taken from King Tut's tomb by robbers 3,000 years ago. But no evidence was found that anyone besides the robbers took anything.

3. AN IRON DAGGER WAS FOUND IN THE TOMB STRAPPED TO KING TUT'S BODY. THE IRON COULD HAVE COME FROM A METEORITE.

An iron dagger was found in the fabrics wrapped around King Tut's body. But Egyptians did not begin to work with iron metal for another 500 years.

So how did King Tut come to have an iron dagger? Experts think it may have been a gift from a king outside of Egypt. One possible source was a meteorite. Meteorites are pieces of space rock that reach Earth. They often contain iron.

THE MYTH

ROBBERS WERE THE ONLY ONES TO TAKE ITEMS FROM KING TUT'S TOMB AFTER HIS BURIAL.

There is strong evidence that Howard Carter took some items from King Tut's tomb during the **excavation**. One object is an **amulet** Carter gave to Sir Alan Gardiner, a member of the excavation team, in 1934. Carter claimed it was not from the tomb. But a member of the Egyptian Museum in Cairo said that it perfectly matched other objects from King Tut's tomb. Experts think it's likely that Carter didn't think it was wrong to take some small items and give them as gifts.

Howard Carter

More than 100 years ago, the world was amazed at the discovery of King Tut's tomb. From this famous find grew many myths. How many myths did you spot?

A small coffin in the tomb held King Tut's mummified liver.

GLOSSARY

amulet (AM-yoo-let)—a small charm believed to protect the wearer from harm

archaeologist (ar-kee-OL-uh-jist)—a person who learns about the past by digging up old buildings or objects and studying them

artifact (AR-tuh-fakt)—an object made by human beings, especially a tool or weapon used in the past

chariot (CHAYR-ee-uht)—a two-wheeled fighting platform used in ancient times that was usually pulled by a horse

curse (KURS)—an evil spell meant to harm someone

economy (i-KAH-nuh-mee)—the ways in which a country handles its money and resources

embalm (im-BALM)—to preserve a dead body so it does not decay

evidence (EV-uh-duhnss)—information, items, and facts that help prove something to be true or false

excavation (ek-skuh-VAY-shuhn)—the process of digging something out

misconception (mis-kuhn-SEP-shuhn)—a wrong or inaccurate idea

READ MORE

Enz, Tammy. *The Science in King Tut's Tomb*. North Mankato, MN: Capstone, 2021.

Fleming, Candace. *The Curse of the Mummy: Uncovering Tutankhamun's Tomb*. New York: Scholastic Focus, 2021.

Gieseke, Tyler. *King Tut*. Minneapolis: Pop!, 2022.

INTERNET SITES

DK Findout!: Tutankhamun
dkfindout.com/us/history/ancient-egypt/tutankhamun

Kiddle: Tutankhamun Facts for Kids
kids.kiddle.co/Tutankhamun

National Geographic Kids: Tutankhamun Facts!
natgeokids.com/uk/discover/history/egypt/tutankhamun-facts

INDEX

Abd el-Rassul, Hussein, 16, 17
afterlife, 22, 23, 26
Akhenaten, 6, 7
annex, 11
antechamber, 11, 15

burial chamber, 11, 13, 23

Carter, Howard, 4, 14, 15, 16, 18, 20, 24, 28
CT scans, 24
curses, 19, 20, 21

fire, 19

gods, 7, 8

hidden rooms, 10, 12

iron daggers, 27

Lord Carnarvon, 14, 15, 19, 20, 21

oils, 18, 19

robbers, 15, 27, 28

sandals, 26
shabtis, 22
steps, 11, 14, 15, 16

Thebes, 7, 8, 9
treasury, 11

X-rays, 22, 24

ABOUT THE AUTHOR

Carol Kim is the author of several fiction and nonfiction books for kids. She enjoys researching and uncovering little-known facts and sharing what she learns with young readers. Carol lives in Austin, Texas, with her family. Learn more about her and her latest books at her website, CarolKimBooks.com.